Mary Kom

"People used to say that boxing is for men and not for women and I thought I will show them some day. I promised myself and I proved myself."

–Mary Kom

It has been rightly said that those who want to fly high do not need strong wings, but strong determination. This statement suits boxer Mary Kom appropriately. Known as 'Magnificent Mary,' Mary Kom belongs to Manipur. Boxing may not exactly be to the fancy of women, but Mary Kom has, by her own admission, shown that gender is immaterial if one has the will to succeed. Having won

Mary Kom smashing opponent with her famous punch

With her husband and two kids

several awards, she is the pride of the country today. Significantly, she is the mother of three children. Mary Kom struck a perfect balance between her family responsibilities and her career in sports and achieved commendable feats. She is a five-time World Boxing Champion and the only woman boxer to have won a medal in each one of the six world championships. She is the only Indian woman boxer to have qualified for the 2012 Summer Olympics, competing in

Mary Kom with her close family, her two sons in inset

the flyweight (51 kg) category and winning the bronze medal.

MC Mary Kom was born to poor parents Kangathei in Churachanpur district in Manipur. Her father was a farmer. Since she came from a poor family, Mary Kom could not spell out her dreams initially. When she did finally make her decision to become a pugilist, people were taken aback because boxing was considered a predominantly male sport. Mary Kom was, however, determined to make it. She

Proud Mother

Receiving a cheque in a resplendentfunction to honour her

completed her primary education from Loktak Christian Model High School and St. Xavier Catholic School. She then moved to Adimjati High School in Imphal. When she failed to pass her examinations, she decided to take her examinations from the National Institute of Open Schooling. This proved a boon in disguise as she got more time to practise the sport she was interested in.

Though she was fascinated with boxing from her childhood, it was only after she saw a group of girls practising at the Khuman Lampak Stadium in Manipur that she grew

Receiving a cheque of Rs. 10 lakh after winning Medal in Olympics

more curious about the sport. She took up the sport in right earnest and did not stop till she achieved her aim.

Mary Kom's ideal was Manipur's Dingko Singh and when the latter won a gold medal at the 1998 Bangkok Asian Games, she was convinced that she too could make it by dint of hard work and practise. It was initially difficult to get the support of the members of her family, but Mary Kom soon succeeded in convincing them of her intent. Mary Kom

Mary Kom with Union Sports Minister Ajay Maken and Olympics Medal Winners

believes that support from one's family is a must for success. She gives all the credit to her father Mangte Tonpa Kom and mother Mangte Akham Kom for their encouragement which eventually made her what she is today.

After 2000, Mary Kom took to full-time professional boxing. After she won the National Women's Boxing Championship in 2001, there was no looking back. She was given the 'Arjun Award' in 2004 and the 'Padma Sree' in 2006. In July, 2009, she was chosen for the top award in sports, the 'Rajiv Gandhi Khel Ratna Award' and was named the 'Woman Player of the Year' by Sahara Khel Puraskar in 2010. The Limca Book of Records also honoured her with the

Honourable President Shri Pranab Mukherji felicitates Mary Kom

'People of the Year.'

In the meanwhile, Mary Kom married Onler Kom and gave birth to twins. Though she was caught up in her household chores, she was getting impatient to participate in the Olympics. With the blessings of a supportive husband, she returned to the ring in 2008. As she toned up with regular practise, she kept training young children in the sport.

The London Olympics opened the door to women pugilists for the first time and this was an opportunity Mary

Receiving 'Rajiv Gandhi Khel Ratan Puraskar' Sports Award from the Prime Minister Dr. Manmohan Singh

Kom did not want to miss. When asked about her preparations for the London Olympics, Mary Kom said, "I was to take part in the 51-kg flyweight category and had to put on 5-6 kg of weight. This was a tough call as adding fat is easy, but gaining muscles is difficult..."

While on the Olympics tour, Mary Kom had to stay away from her children for some time. Her twins could watch their mother on television, but they missed her. About this, Mary Kom said, "I missed my children, but I was determined to do something for my country. I had to earn a name for the country at the Olympics which was my dream. I could not

Mary Kom'smoment of exhilarationafter winning Olympics Medal

A proud winner displaying her Medal

stay away from it..."

The London competition was tough. Mary Kom had to face strong contestants to win her bronze medal. On returning to India to a warm welcome, she said, "Winning a medal at the Olympics is an honour. I am indebted to the people of my country for their cooperation. I am glad people know me now."

The London Olympics win made Mary Kom a household name as she was featured extensively in the media. As she made headlines, Raj Kundra, husband of Bollywood actress, Shilpa Shetty made Mary Kom the brand ambassador for his

Proud moment for MaryKomon being declared a winner

Super Fight League. Mary Kom walked the ramp with several Bollywood stars. She also travelled to Mizwa, the village of poet-lyricist Kaifi Azmi and took part in an event of the Mizwa Foundation.

Soon, filmmaker Sanjay Leela Bhansali will start shooting for a film on Mary Kom's life. The script has been written by Umang Kumar who met Mary Kom before she left

Mary Kom posing for photographers

Receiving flower bouquet from a child at a function to felicitate her

Mary Kom making the victory sign

to participate in the Olympics. It was only after that Mary Kom agreed that Kumar began to script her life. Asked about his film, Bhansali said, "I was amazed to hear Mary Kom's success story. A mother of two who faced many odds in life and then made it as a winner in the Olympics – that itself is a source of inspiration. Mary Kom truly has all the attributes of a champion. There are but only a few woman boxers. I am excited about the film myself. It should hit the screens by the end of this year or latest by early 2014."

Famous Bollywood director Sanjay Leela Bhansali posing with Mary Kom. Also in the photois Priyanka Chopra who will play the role of Mary Kom in a forthcoming feature film

Mary Kom is an inspiration for such women stuck in their household chores who think they had no time to participate in anything other than in family matters. Here is a woman who took care of her family and also realized her dream. Mary teaches us that there is nothing impossible in life and you can fly on the wings of your determination.